UP NORTH

GETAWAYS OF MINNESOTA AND WISCONSIN

JON KREYE

DEDICATION

To Laken - may you always have a passion
and appreciation for the outdoors, the
beauty of creation around you, and time
spent adventuring with your family. I am
always proud of you.

ACKNOWLDGEMENTS

I would like to acknowledge my parents
Dave and Barb for instilling the importance
and appreciation of travel, the outdoors,
and spending time with loved ones in
cabins from a young age. I would like to
acknowledge my beautiful bride, Cambell,
for loving me through my busy travel
schedule and allowing me to do what
I love everyday - you are the best. I would
like to thank my uncle Paul Madsen for
encouraging me to be bold and to
self-publish a book, and for all of the
advice given. Finally, I would like to thank
my God for his enduring love, forgiveness,
and grace, which is the most important
gift I've received in life.

TABLE OF CONTENTS

INTRODUCTION

Cabins, cottages, short term rentals, lake houses, resorts, Airbnb's, getaways. There are many words for the places we choose to escape to, but their essence is all the same - a place for peace. A place to get away from the hustle and bustle of everyday life. A place to be still. A place to make memories. A place to have fun. A place for family. A place to recreate. A place to recharge.

Upon arriving at a cabin the stress seems to fade away, the food tastes a little better, the birds chirp a little louder, and the traffic is a little quieter. The camera roll fills up a little quicker and the memories linger a little longer. Time moves a little slower and each breath is a little deeper. Life is a little simpler.

The cabin in America has long been a symbol of our love for freedom and our need for rest. We seem to have an innate urge to get away from the rest of the world and slow down. Today's getaway is more of a necessity than ever with our ever-present technology, fast-paced culture, hurried mentality, mental health issues, and digital driven lives. The getaway - whether it is a weeklong summer trip, a regular place to escape year-round, or a weekend excursion once a year is an integral part of Midwest culture. It is a staple of the people's lives who live in this land.

Minnesota and Wisconsin are full of lakes, forests, and secluded beauty. These two Midwest states have become destinations for those who want to experience the pristine beauty of lake country and the north woods.

Growing up in Wisconsin in an outdoor loving family meant visiting a rental cabin up north for a week each summer. For us, up north usually meant somewhere at least a two hour drive by car north of home. Up north is a term you will hear a lot around the Midwest. It means different things to different people, but usually it centers around getaways in the woods or on the water somewhere north of home. It amazes me how a simple term about changing latitude can create a true mindset shift. Being up north is intertwined with the feelings of inner peace and relaxation we often find at a getaway.

The pattern of time spent at different vacation homes up north in my childhood instilled a desire to continue this tradition throughout my life. Little did I know it would one day become one of the most compelling passions of my life and lead me to a career focused on capturing unique stays across the country.

Each of the photographs in this book embody fond and vivid memories for me. While looking at the images, you may be taken into these spaces as well, even if just for a moment. I encourage you to slow down as you flip through the pages ahead - imagining the sights, sounds, smells, and emotions you would feel if you were immersed in the space your eyes are looking at. I hope this inspires you to get back to your oasis wherever it may be and maybe even plan a trip to one of the getaways you'll find in this book. Wherever up north is to you - may you find peace and rest there.

Happy trails.

MODERN GETAWAYS

CLASSIC GETAWAYS

93

UNIQUE GETAWAYS

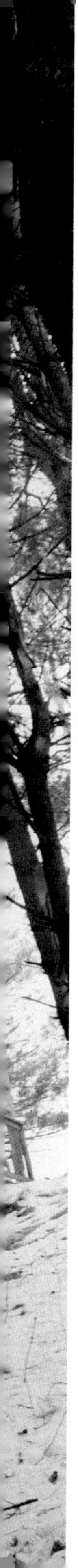

INDEX

ABOUT THE AUTHOR
+ PHOTOGRAPHER

Jon Kreye is an award winning adventure photographer based in Minnesota, USA. Inspired by his love for adventure, nature, and cabins, his passion for experiencing and photographing unique stays started at a young age. Jon has stayed in some of the most unique and highly desired rental properties across the country including shipping container cabins, treehouses, dome homes, private islands, yurts, barn homes, and more. This is Jon's first book, compiling his work in one volume is a proud accomplishment for him. When he is not photographing cabins he enjoys time with his wife and daughter at their family cabin, on the trail, and at the lake.

Follow his adventures on Instagram **@jonkreye**.

Made in the USA
Las Vegas, NV
25 October 2024

56a16c76-de4a-4e69-9b72-a40133f917f8R01